Table of Contents

Chapter 1

Raw Holiday Survival Guide

Fall and winter holidays are a time for fun, family, sharing, love, generosity, excitement, lights, anticipation, celebrating, parties, cinnamon and nutmeg, costumes, decorations, and more. The evidence is easy to spot. As fall begins, you start seeing holiday decorations hanging around your favorite department stores. I look forward to this time of year, all year long.

During all of this excitement however, time naturally flies and seems to run through your fingers quickly. It can be a time of stress for some because of increasingly busy and hectic schedules. Moreover, there tends to be a lot of unnecessary sickness because people are filling their bodies with toxins, not getting enough exercise or rest, and congregating a lot indoors to stay warm from the chilly weather. All of these things make a cozy breeding ground for illness.

To make sure your holidays are filled with as much happiness, health and fun as possible, I've written this book to be your survival guide. Follow the tips and tricks presented here, gobble up plenty of fresh organic raw vegan food (use these recipes as some of your staples), find time to relax *and* exercise, and have the best holiday season ever. At a time when the rest of the world is packing on pounds and clogging their arteries with all kinds of yule tide crud, you'll be filling your body with super healthy and energizing food – at the time of year when you need energy and health the most!

Succeeding with the Raw vegan lifestyle during the holidays has never been easier. With a few tips and tricks, some simple organization, a relaxed state of mind, and terrific recipes, you are sure to love the fall and winter holidays more than ever. The key is to begin early with your thinking and planning. This way, you have a chance to plan properly, figure out what foods you will make, try some great recipes in anticipation, and practice them (so you can show them off at family gatherings!).

Expectations Are Important

It's important to manage expectations, both your own, as well as those of your family (whether they are eating raw or not). Expectations for what you are going to eat at holiday dinners, expectations for what you'll serve or bring as your dish to pass (describing it realistically is important, instead of naming it something that makes people expect the traditional, Standard American Diet version), and expectations about your lifestyle. It helps to start thinking about and discussing these things with family and friends sooner than later.

October is a great time to start thinking about what you will tell your family and friends. Let them know how you'll be approaching the holidays with your Raw vegan lifestyle. This helps you, your family, and friends prepare. For me, it's important that no one is "put out" by my lifestyle. Therefore, I always tell people that I will bring my own food to a gathering or party and that the host or hostess does not have to worry about me. Additionally, I always offer to bring a nice fresh raw vegan dish to pass, so others can sample something from my lifestyle.

Another great reason to plan early is so you can prepare some delicious raw vegan foods in advance (for example: raw vegan desserts that you can make in October and November – or earlier – they typically freeze well for 6–12 months). Then, you'll have them on hand to snack on, or take with you to parties, so they help you "stay Raw." This is also very helpful if you need to bring a dish and you're short on time, because you'll already have it made. It's so hectic in November and December that you'll be glad you thought of these things ahead of time.

Be Prepared

Consider preparation as your "armor." Protect yourself and make your life easier by having your food plans thought out in advance. And, do this *before* the season gets too busy. You might be attending parties, spending time decorating and shopping, and overall having more to do than normal. Be prepared and think ahead. One way I handle this is to have food to take with me all the time. I like to pack snacks for my purse and car. This way, I know I have something to eat at all times and I never worry. This eases my mind and makes me feel relaxed.

Another common worry is how to stay true to the Raw diet with so many holiday parties to attend. Again, it's about simple preparation and forethought. When I attend parties, the following are examples of things I do before going so that I set myself up to win. *No appetizer tray or dessert table will get the best of me. Heck no! I won't give that junk a second thought.* Before you attend a holiday party or event, consider doing one of the following:

- Drink a green smoothie, or
- Eat 1–2 pieces of fruit, or
- Drink a protein shake, or
- Eat your meal before leaving your house

Another option is to bring your food to the party. If I'm going to a party at work or at someone's home, I have absolutely no problem bringing my own snacks or food to eat. I am responsible for my own health so I act accordingly. To make it more comfortable and relaxed, I usually let someone know ahead of time (if necessary) so there aren't questions when I arrive. I keep it very relaxed and low key… like it's "no big deal and I do it all the time." The best part is when I bring extras for people to sample, and they love it! That's fun.

The best way to accomplish this, if you're tight on time, is to have some foods already made, stored in your freezer and ready to thaw. Things like crackers, corn chips, cheese dips, granola bars, flax/chia breads, and desserts all freeze nicely and last a long time. Yes, fresh is usually best, but having some frozen goods on hand can be great. So, go ahead and start making a few things in October and November (or before) to freeze and store.

It's Easy

Be organized and make life easier. Every week, take an hour or two to plan your food for the week. Get out your favorite recipes, write your shopping list, and plan on your calendar "when" you're going to make "what" (I keep a completely separate kitchen calendar to plan my food prep). If you need to soak nuts and seeds or, "soak and dehydrate them," look ahead on the calendar and plan when you'll be doing these steps. You should also take the time to do this early on for planning any events you'll be hosting.

Afraid you'll be way too busy to do any food prep for yourself? No worries. Make it super easy on yourself and order Raw vegan meals online and have them delivered to you. This can also be very helpful when you're traveling to parts of the country where you might have a hard time making your own food (or if you're simply too busy). There are some terrific sources. As of writing this, Rawvolution.com, PureMarketExpress.com, and PureRawCafe.com all deliver raw vegan meals nationwide.

If you know you'll be spending your holidays somewhere that you can prepare Raw vegan food, but you're unsure as to whether you'll have organic ingredients available to you, then you can order that online, too! Check out these two fantastic sources: BoxedGreens.com and DiamondOrganics.com.

Exercise and Rest

Now is one of the most important times to make sure you're exercising and getting enough rest. Yes, I consider long shopping trips, for holiday gifts, great exercise, especially if you're carrying a fair share of bags. If you're not shopping at the malls and you're doing a lot of your shopping online (like me), then make time to get to the gym. And, if you don't have a gym membership, then a fast way to get exercise is by jumping rope, taking a quick jog (even if it's only around the block), or jumping on a rebounder (if you don't have one of these – now is the perfect time to ask for one). These exercises are superior for helping you get your lymph flowing. *Be sure to always check with a physician before embarking on a physical exercise program.*

Rest and adequate sleep are also important. You don't want to be frazzled at this time of year, and it's known to do that to people. There is going to be more traffic than normal on the road and in the stores. One way to make sure you're not "on edge" is to be rested and relaxed. Recognize the holidays as a busy time of year and embrace it. Realize that you're doing so much good for your body by eating raw organic plant-based foods, getting exercise and rest, and that you're setting yourself up for optimal health. That alone should make you smile from ear to ear.

My Best Friends During the Holidays

This is the time of year when you'll find yourself surrounded by family, friends, co-workers, and loved ones who may not take as good care of themselves as you do. As a result, many people typically become ill during the holidays and the flu runs rampant. With some extra precautions, you could find yourself breezing through the holidays (setting an example of pure health along the way) even though you are surrounded by sneezing, coughing, bloated and puffy people. There are a few things I do to help keep my immune system stronger during this time of year, and I like to think of them as my "best friends" during the holidays:

- Extra Greens – I drink *lots* of fresh green juice ("Plant Blood"), green smoothies, and I sometimes add a green powder to them. (I prefer *Vitamineral Green* powder and *Amazing Grass Wheat Grass* powder, check out KristensRaw.com/store for details.) Greens help alkalize the body and they're loaded with superior nutrition. Be sure to get plenty of them in your diet.

- Hydration – If I'm drinking everything that I just mentioned above *and* eating a High Raw (or all Raw) diet, then I should be well hydrated. However, it doesn't hurt to keep the fluids coming. A great way I easily add more water to my daily diet is to start and end every day with a nice cup of warm water with a squeeze of fresh organic lemon in it.

- Probiotics – During a time of year that I usually find myself busier than normal, possibly more stressed, and surrounded by others who are likely to be sick... I take precautions and arm myself by taking probiotics. This way, I have plenty of friendly bacteria in my digestive system helping me stay healthy.

- Fermented Foods – Fermented foods such as raw (unpasteurized) sauerkraut and kim-chi (pronounced "kim chee") are quite popular around the world. They're a staple in my diet year round. I love fermented foods because they are low in calories, have plenty of fiber, and they're filled with a rich content of vitamins and minerals. Plus, they help build up and maintain friendly bacteria in my body. All of these benefits are important… especially around the holidays. I like to make my own sauerkraut from freshly picked organic cabbage that I get from the farmer's market. It takes about a month (or longer if desired) to ferment in my stoneware fermentation pot, so I make plenty of this when cabbage is in season. Then, I store it in my refrigerator for the months to come. If you don't want to make your own, you can purchase delicious raw, organic, unpastuerized sauerkraut online from Gold Mine Natural Foods (GoldMineNaturalFood.com), from Rejuvenative Foods (Rejuvenative.com), or sometimes Whole Foods Market has it.

Staying Warm During the Holidays

A great way that I stay warm during the holidays, if I'm spending them in chilly parts of the world (other than bundling up in a nice comfy sweater and squishy socks), is with a lovely cup of organic miso soup. Although miso soup is not "Raw," it is "Living" and contains natural digestive enzymes. I love that within the first few sips I feel my body warming from head to toe. There are a number of brands available, but there is one that truly stands out – it's my all-time favorite and I highly recommend it – South River Miso (it's organic and they even have soy-free varieties if you're interested). Check out their website at SouthRiverMiso.com.

Practice Makes Perfect

During the holidays, you'll no doubt be attending various family and friend gatherings, if you're not hosting one yourself. Now is the time to shine! Use the following recipes to make fabulous food that you can take to parties. And, if you're hosting your own, then look no further because you have everything you need right here. If you're not great in the kitchen then my advice is to make these once or twice before your holiday gatherings for practice. Remember, you want to shine and show off these delicious raw vegan foods.

If you're tight on time during the holidays (like most of us are), then a few of these can be made ahead of time, frozen, and life is easier. I have noted which recipes freeze well at the end of each recipe.

Treats as Gifts

I love giving out little holiday raw vegan treats as fun gifts for family, friends and co-workers. Raw vegan chocolates, desserts, and cookies are great for this. You can go to your local crafts store and buy cute bags and decorations. Make some raw vegan candies or cookies, wrap them up, and hand them out. Such fun! If you don't have time to make these things, then there are plenty of options available online or in stores such as Whole Foods Market. For example, a terrific gift for a friend or loved one is a bag of *Laughing Giraffe's Snackaroons*. (They are heavenly!)

Don't forget gifts for your mail carrier, hairdresser, pet groomer, teachers, doctor, veterinarian, etc. – *what a great way to introduce more people to Raw Vegan Foods!*

Speaking of Gifts… Let's Talk About Wrapping

Did you know that Americans spend an estimated $2.7 billion annually on ribbons, paper, and bows, and almost all of those goods end up in the dumpster?

It's no secret that eating a raw vegan diet makes a difference for our planet, whether you're 100% or not (every little bit counts!). But, I don't stop with my diet. I say that I "live" the raw vegan lifestyle… so I incorporate food and the environment as priorities in my life and you should, too.

With the holidays coming upon us, let's help save our planet by taking a close look at gift wrapping (and all year for that matter, i.e. birthdays, anniversaries, etc). Here are some ideas for Green gift wrapping over the holidays and to use year round.

This year, try re-purposing stuff. Eco-stylist Danny Seo, author of the book *Simply Green Giving*, wrote, "It's amazing what you can find at Goodwill. Vintage fabrics, wallpaper, and sweaters all make great wrapping – just look for rich textures." Sometimes the wrap will serve as part of the gift, as in the case of a belt or scarf used as a bow.

Here are some more ideas that you can use for wrapping paper: Magazines, newsprint, comics, and so on make cool gift wrap as well. You can also reuse gift wrap from previous years. Get creative and find ads that "speak" to the person you're giving the gift to; this makes it extra special, fun and personal.

If anybody looks at you funny, just say, "I'm doin' the Green thing." People not only get it, they usually appreciate it, or comment on how they might consider doing it themselves.

A Great Gift for You

Here is an idea that you might like to try. For the holidays I ask my family and friends to go vegan for five days, as their gift to me. (Honestly, asking them to go Raw would be too much of a stretch.) With the money they won't be spending on me, I provide them with a shopping list so they can buy a few staples to last them the week (For example: fresh organic fruits and vegetables, coconut yogurt, rice or hemp milk, organic soy butter, non-GMO tofu, beans or grains, and maybe some frozen vegan foods, etc.). I give them simple and delicious recipes for vegan dishes (as well as a few raw dishes), a list of restaurants in their area where they can order great vegan food (I use the Internet for areas that I'm not familiar with), as well as my recommendations for breakfasts, lunches and dinners. I give them everything they could possibly need for making the five days easy and fun. I also give them a free vegetarian starter kit from "GoVeg" (GoVeg.com) that I preorder to arrive in time.

Have a Fun Raw Food Prep Party

Are you planning a holiday party? How about having a party with very little work on your part? What's even better is that you'll get more people interested in your Raw lifestyle with ease. Are you intrigued? Here is what you do – set the date, invite your guests, tell everyone to bring an apron, plan a fantastic, easy and fun raw menu, buy the ingredients, print the recipes so everyone has a copy to take home, put out your favorite raw books for optional browsing, play fun music, drink organic vegan wine (optional, but I offer it at my parties), and have a great time. Your guests will make the recipes one by one, taking turns with the steps, while you guide them and talk about all the amazing benefits of eating raw.

One of the reasons people are intimidated by raw food is simply not knowing enough about it, such as *how* to make it, *what* to make, and most importantly, *why*. By now, I'm sure "you" know it's really simple, but your family and friends might not realize this. Now (or any time of year, of course) is a great time to have a party where you gather friends at your house and teach them how to make Raw food. Teaching people about Raw vegan food in a relaxed and fun atmosphere is the best way to get more people interested. Promise your guests a lot of fun with delicious food to eat. Who could turn that down? This will be a party that everyone will remember because everyone will have a great time and enjoy truly exceptional food!

Here is another idea for a party. If you are hosting a large party where you have plenty of food to prepare, enlist the help of friends beforehand and make it a party of fun. People love to help. Promise them a sampling of healthy raw vegan food and tons of fun.

Whatever the reason is for having a party, this is a fantastic way to help others learn about Raw vegan food.

The Holidays Will Be a Breeze

Navigating the fall and winter holidays has never been such a breeze. You simply need to spend a little time planning and getting organized in advance. I recommend that you start this every year in October by planning out the foods you'd like to have made and frozen, menus for parties or gatherings, the ingredients you'll need for everything over the next couple of months (you might need to order nuts, seeds, raw chocolate, etc), as well as getting prepped for gifts you'd like to give people regarding raw treats, as well as receive (having people temporarily go vegan as their gift to you).

So, without further ado… I'm thrilled to share the following delicious and highly nutritious raw vegan holiday recipes that you and your family are sure to enjoy… (during the holidays *and* all year long). What makes the following recipes special for the holidays? Well, they either have holiday flavors (or ingredients), they are made from ingredients that are the colors of the holidays, or they are recipes that pack some extra nutritional punch to help support your immune system during a hectic time of year. With recipes as delicious, nutritious, decadent and fun, you won't miss the other stuff.

To begin… keep the following in mind when making foods for the holidays:

Holiday Foods & Colors!

Think about colors with your food to make special holiday meals. Here are some examples:

- Fall colors with fresh vegetables that are orange, dark red, and yellow.
- Zucchini pasta marinara makes a lovely holiday meal with the bright green and red colors.
- Chopped tomatoes drizzled with raw olive oil, a little Himalayan crystal salt, and topped with fragrant fresh herbs such as rosemary, dill and basil.
- Coloring coconut with beet juice is a great way to add color to your dishes or as a fun garnish. Here is a simple recipe to try:

Red Holiday Coconut

Here is a quick and easy way to add color to your coconut. This is beautiful sprinkled on desserts, salads, or entrees.

1/4 cup dried coconut, shredded and unsweetened

2 tablespoons fresh beet juice

Stir the coconut and beet juice together in a bowl. Spread the mixture onto a dehydrator sheet fitted with a ParaFlexx non-stick sheet. Dehydrate at 105 degrees F until dry (6–12 hours or more). Store in a glass mason jar in your refrigerator for up to two months or in your freezer for 6–12 months.

Chapter 2

Delicious & Nutritious Beverages

— ANTHELME BRILLAT-SAVARIN

I'm starting the recipes with a chapter dedicated to nutritious beverages, because it's important to stay properly hydrated on a daily basis, especially around the holidays. I further enhance my health during this time by drinking plenty of freshly made green juices (or *Plant Blood*, as I like to call them) and smoothies. This is one of the best ways to load your body up with extra nutrients, which is something we need lots of during the holiday season.

Sweetie Tart Plant Blood

Yield 1 serving

I lovingly call my green juices "Plant Blood" for fun. Here is an amazingly delicious and super nutritious recipe that is loaded with vitamins, minerals, and antioxidants.

1 beet

1 head broccoli florets

1 lemon, peeled

1 small/medium pineapple, peeled*

1 inch fresh ginger

Juice all of the ingredients and enjoy.

* For extra nutrition, be sure to include the core of the pineapple when juicing.

Festive Party Time Juice

Yield 2 cups

This is a deliciously fun and sassy juice… perfect for the season with nutritious cranberries and apples. Yum! The color is vibrant and gorgeous. The way to know you're getting loads of nutrients is by consuming brightly colored raw vegan foods… this is a perfect example!

2 cups fresh cranberries

2 large apples (select a sweet variety)

1/8 inch fresh ginger (or more)

Juice all of the ingredients and enjoy in sassy and festive wine glasses.

Optional:

- You can add 1/2–1 teaspoon raw agave nectar to sweeten it up a bit, but I prefer it as a fun, more tart-like beverage – preferring the taste of the fresh cranberries to come through.

Festive Party Time Juice

Raspberry Spinach Smoothie

Yield 1 serving

Even though the end product isn't necessarily a holiday color, before you blend the mixture it is! This is a great smoothie for any time of the day because it's loaded with energy, nutrition and lots of fiber.

1/2 cup water (more if desired)

2 cups spinach, packed

1 cup raspberries

1 banana, peeled

1/8 teaspoon vanilla extract

tiny pinch nutmeg

Blend all of the ingredients until smooth.

Spiced Green Smoothie

Yield 3 cups (1–2 servings)

Kale is a staple in my diet because it is a nutrient powerhouse. It's filled with loads of vitamins, minerals, and phytochemicals. The funny thing is that when I first introduced my husband to a smoothie with kale it in, he couldn't believe it. He said, "I thought that stuff was just for decoration around salad bars." He knows better now and proudly boasts to his friends about how great kale is. Bring on the kale!

1 1/2 cups water

3 leaves curly kale

1 pear, cored and chopped

1 apple, cored and chopped

2 cloves

Blend all of the ingredients until smooth.

Sweet Chlorophyll Surprise

Getting plenty of chlorophyll into your diet is very important around the holidays (and all year long!). The wheat grass in this delicious recipe is perfect for just that. And, the pineapple is a good source of manganese, vitamins C, B6, B1, as well as copper.

1 cup water

2 bananas, peeled

1 cup pineapple, peeled, cored and chopped (or leave in the core)

1 tablespoon powdered wheat grass

1 teaspoon ginger, freshly grated

Blend all of the ingredients until smooth.

Mauve Majesty Smoothie

Yield 3 1/2 cups

This is one of my favorite smoothie recipes. It's a beautiful, vibrant color, which shows off all of the antioxidants. And, the flavor is fantastic.

Raspberries – these are so good for you! I am a huge cheerleader for organic raspberries, so I gobble them up with glee. They contain vitamins C, B2, B3, folate, magnesium, potassium, as well as tons of fiber. Research suggests that raspberries may offer some cancer protective properties because of all of the phytonutrients they contain.

1 cup water

2 cups broccoli florets

1 1/2 cups raspberries

2 bananas, peeled

1 1/2 teaspoons ginger, freshly grated

pinch cinnamon

Blend all of the ingredients until smooth and creamy.

Holiday Time Breakfast Smoothie

Yield 2 cups

A wonderful way to start your morning during the holidays is with this super simple and quick breakfast holiday flavored smoothie. And, it's quite a pretty color (*ha ha*… I'm such a girl!).

1 cup water

2 bananas, peeled

1 cup carrots, chopped

3/4 teaspoon pumpkin pie spice

Blend all of the ingredients until smooth and creamy. Carrots take a little longer to get smooth so you might want to blend this a little longer than normal.

Lively Breakfast Smoothie

This smoothie is delicious, fun, and has such a beautiful vibrant color to it! It's a terrific way to start your day.

Though this particular recipe doesn't have either holiday colors or flavors in it, as I wrote in the chapter introduction… it's important to consume plenty of nutritious liquids during the holidays so I'm including plenty of nutrient dense beverage recipes to accomplish just that!

The broccoli, banana, and yellow bell peppers offer you so many vitamins and minerals. This smoothie is super nutrition in a cup.

1 cup water

1 heaping cup broccoli florets

1 banana, peeled

2 cups yellow bell pepper, chopped

Blend all of the ingredients until smooth.

Pillowy Vanilla Cashew Milk

Yield 2 cups

This is the perfect comfort beverage for those times you want something sweet and satiating, and to prevent you from gorging on something not-so-good for you during the holidays. And, it just might be the perfect milk to leave out for Santa Claus on Christmas Eve.

I use the word "pillowy" in the title because every sip is soft, smooth, and comfy… just like the perfect pillow.

1/2 cup raw cashews

1–1 1/4 cups water

2 soft medjool dates, pitted

2 teaspoons chia seeds

1 teaspoon lucuma powder

1/4 teaspoon vanilla extract

Place the cashews in a bowl and cover with enough water by about an inch. Let them soak for 1 hour. Drain off the water and give them a quick rinse. Blend everything together until wonderfully smooth and creamy. Pillowy Vanilla Cashew Milk freezes well.

Creamy Dreamy Eggless Nog

See photo with "Deck the Halls" Pistachio Cranberry Cookies, Ch. 4.

Yield 4 cups

When I first gave this to my husband to taste, I asked, "What does this remind you of?" He immediately exclaimed, "Eggnog!" – *but there's no dairy or eggs!*

1/2 cup raw pecans

1/2 cup raw macadamia nuts

1/4 cup raisins

7 dates, pitted

2 1/2 cups water

3 cloves, crushed

1/2 teaspoon vanilla extract

1/2 teaspoon rum extract

1/2 teaspoon cinnamon

1/4 teaspoon cardamom

1/4 teaspoon nutmeg

1/4 teaspoon ginger powder

pinch Himalayan crystal salt

Place the pecans in a bowl and cover with enough water by about an inch. Let them soak for 6–8 hours. Drain off the water and give them a quick rinse. Place the macadamia nuts in a bowl and cover with enough water by about an inch. Let them soak for 1–2 hours. Drain off the water and give them a quick rinse. Place the raisins and dates in a bowl and cover with enough water by 1-2 inches. Let them soak for 1 hour. Drain off the water and give them a quick rinse.

Blend all of the ingredients together until smooth and creamy. Enjoy this served in lovely wine goblets or glasses. Creamy Dreamy Eggless Nog freezes well.

Chapter 3

Entrée, Sides, Salads, Soup & Breakfast

— SOCRATES

This chapter offers delicious, fun, and fabulous foods to keep the holiday spirit going strong all season long (or heck, all year long if you make some of these year round like I do).

"Boo!" Halloween Hummus

Yield 2 1/4 cups

Due to its blackish color, this hummus is loads of fun for Halloween. I love serving it with bright orange colored vegetables to make it complete.

2 zucchini, peeled and chopped

1/2 cup fresh lemon juice

2 cloves garlic

1 1/2 teaspoons cumin

1 teaspoon Himalayan crystal salt

1/4 teaspoon coriander

3/4 cup raw black tahini*

Blend all of the ingredients in your blender until creamy. Serve with sliced orange bell peppers or carrot sticks. This recipe freezes well.

* Online retailer Living Tree Community has black tahini. You can find a link to their website at KristensRaw.com/store. You can also find it at some Whole Foods Markets.

Kristen Suzanne's Raw Harvest Soup

This is a beautiful and creamy soup that I love making all year long. (It's one of my family's favorites!) During the fall holidays, I make the "variation" recipe (noted below) by adding the coriander and pumpkin spice. Delicious!

1 cup water

1 large zucchini, chopped

2 medium tomatoes, quartered

3 stalks celery, chopped

2 cups carrots, chopped

2 soft dates, pitted

1 clove garlic

2 teaspoons Himalayan crystal salt

1 tablespoon onion powder

1/2 teaspoon black pepper

1/2 cup flax oil or raw olive oil

Blend all of the ingredients, except the oil, on high speed in your blender until really creamy (approximately one minute – I prefer this soup to be very creamy). Then, while the blender is running on low speed, add the oil. Continue blending for another minute or so. This will make it slightly warm.

Variations:

- Add 1/2 teaspoon coriander and/or 1/2 teaspoon pumpkin pie spice (awesome!).

Festive Vegetable Mix

This is a fantastic way to dress up vegetables and make them extra delicious. It's a gorgeous side dish for any holiday party.

1/2 cup raw olive oil

3 tablespoons fresh lemon juice

2 teaspoons dried thyme

1 1/2 teaspoons garlic, pressed

1/2 teaspoon onion powder

1/2 teaspoon Himalayan crystal salt

1/4 teaspoon black pepper

2 dashes nutmeg

3 cups zucchini, chopped

3 cups red bell pepper, diced

3/4 cup raw walnuts, chopped

Whisk together the raw olive oil, lemon juice, thyme, garlic, onion powder, salt, pepper and nutmeg in a bowl. Place the chopped zucchini and red bell pepper in an 8 × 8 glass baking dish. Pour the marinade on top and stir to coat everything. Let marinate for an hour, then add the nuts and serve.

Or, if you have a dehydrator, that's even better! Place the marinated veggies in your dehydrator (without the nuts) for about an hour at 130 degrees F to warm them. Lower the temperature to 105 degrees F for another 1–2 hours. Top with nuts and serve. You can make this dish the day before serving. Let it marinate in your refrigerator overnight (without the nuts). Top with nuts prior to serving.

Variations:

- Add dried cherries.

- Replace the raw walnuts with pine nuts, hemp seeds, or pecans.
- Use fresh broccoli florets instead of zucchini.

Holiday Carrot Pear Mash

Yield approximately 3 cups

This is a fun recipe that is easy to make and is great as a side dish. Plus, kids really love it!

3 cups carrots, chopped

2 pears, cored and chopped

2 tablespoons raw agave nectar (or more)

1 1/2 tablespoons fresh lemon or lime juice

1/4 teaspoon Himalayan crystal salt (or more)

1 teaspoon rum or maple extract

1/4 cup dried fruit (cranberries, cherries, golden raisins, or mulberries)

Puree all of the ingredients, except the dried fruit, using a food processor, fitted with the "S" blade. Stir in the dried fruit.

Holiday Morning Porridge

Yield 2 servings

For those of you who miss oatmeal, you're going to love this. It's a creamy, delicious and filling recipe, especially great for serving to your out-of-town guests.

1 cup raw rolled oats*

1/2 cup raw macadamia nuts, unsoaked

1 large banana, peeled (or 1 large apple, cored and chopped)

2 tablespoons raw agave nectar (or 3–4 dates, pitted and chopped)

1/4–1/2 teaspoon pumpkin pie spice

pinch Himalayan crystal salt

2 tablespoons dried cranberries (optional)

Place the oats in a bowl with enough water to cover by about an inch or so. Let them soak like this overnight, on your countertop, covered lightly with a paper towel. The next morning, drain and rinse the oats.

Grind the macadamia nuts until they're coarsely ground, using a food processor, fitted with the "S" blade. Add the remaining ingredients, except for the dried cranberries, and process until smooth. Stir in the dried cranberries and serve immediately. Or, warm in the dehydrator at 130 degrees F for approximately 25–40 minutes prior to serving.

Variations:

- Replace the macadamia nuts with hemp seeds or soaked and dehydrated pecans or walnuts. If using hemp seeds, then skip the grinding step and add them to the food processor with the other ingredients in the following step.
- Replace the dried cranberries with raisins, goji berries, chopped dried apricots, dried cherries or currants.

* NaturalZing.com offers 100% organic fresh raw rolled oats that are cold-

rolled in small batches with special equipment to maintain nutrients.

Red Corn Chips

Yield approximately 50–60 chips, depending on the size you score

This is a neat recipe for corn chips that come out a pretty dark red color, which is perfect for the holidays.

3/4 cup water

5 cups frozen corn (thawed), or use fresh corn cut from the cob*

2 cups yellow bell pepper, seeded and chopped

1/4 cup beet, chopped

2 teaspoons Himalayan crystal salt

3/4 cup flax meal

Blend all of the ingredients, except for the flax meal, until smooth. Transfer to a bowl and stir in the flax meal. Allow the mixture to sit for about five minutes as the flax meal absorbs the vegetable mixture. Spread the mixture onto two dehydrator trays (using an offset spatula for easiest spreading), lined with non-stick ParaFlexx sheets. Score into desired size.

Dehydrate for one hour at 130–140 degrees F. Then, reduce the temperature to 105 degrees F and continue dehydrating another 10 hours. Flip the Red Corn Chips onto dehydrator trays, without ParaFlexx sheets, and peel off the current ParaFlexx sheets being used. Continue dehydrating another 10–14 hours, or until dry. These freeze well.

* Frozen corn is not raw since most frozen vegetables are blanched before being frozen. Fresh is best, but it's not always in season. Therefore, I buy lots of fresh organic corn when it is in season, I cut it from the cobs, and I freeze it with my FoodSaver® – no blanching needed.

Groovy Kale Salad

Yield 4 servings

This is a fun and beautifully colored salad, with rich purple and green curly kale mixed with vibrant vegetables and fruits.

- **1 large bunch purple curly kale**
- **2–3 tablespoons fresh lemon juice**
- **2 tablespoons tamari, wheat-free**
- **2 tablespoons raw olive oil or hemp oil**
- **10 grape or cherry tomatoes, halved**
- **1 red bell pepper, seeded and diced**
- **2 cups carrots, shredded**
- **3/4 cup pineapple, peeled, cored and diced**
- **1 tablespoon ginger, freshly grated**
- **5 soft medjool dates, pitted and chopped**
- **season with salt and pepper, if desired**

Destem the kale. You can leave the more tender parts of the stem (toward the top of each leaf) in the salad, but the harder stems toward the bottom of each leaf should be torn out. Use a knife to chop the kale into small pieces. (Juice the kale stems not used in the salad or throw them into your yard for bunnies to eat.)

Place the kale into a large bowl. Add the lemon juice, tamari, and oil. Massage the mixture thoroughly (a minute or two), and you'll notice the kale shrinking in size and getting juicy. Add the remaining ingredients and give it another couple quick squeezes.

Cranberry Kiwi Relish

This delicious and highly nutritious recipe is refreshing, fun, light, and lively. I can't seem to keep my fork out of the bowl when I make this wonderful recipe!

There are plenty of reasons to add cranberries to your diet, but most people only think about cranberries around the holidays. Cranberries have vitamin C, dietary fiber, vitamin K, manganese, and more. Bring on the fresh, organic cranberries!

2 cups fresh cranberries

2 oranges, peeled, pith removed, seeded and sectioned

2 kiwis, peeled and diced

1/3 cup raw agave nectar, or more to taste

2 tablespoons green onion, minced

2 tablespoons fresh lime juice

1 teaspoon fresh ginger, grated

Process the cranberries and oranges briefly in a food processor, fitted with the "S" blade. Transfer to a bowl and add the other ingredients. Stir by hand.

This is a wonderful salad that is loaded with nutrients. I love eating a big bowl of this and having "I Can't Believe It's Raw" Pumpkin Pie for dessert (see recipe, Chapter 4).

2 medium–large red bell peppers, seeded and chopped

2 medium–large cucumbers, chopped

1/4 cup raisins

1 bag of pre-washed spinach

3/4 cup Rosemary Ranch Dressing (see recipe, below)

Put all of the salad ingredients in a big bowl and toss gently to mix.

Rosemary Ranch Dressing/Dip

Yield 2 cups

This fabulous recipe can be used as a deliciously rich vegetable dip or as a raw, non-dairy creamy dressing. It tends to thicken after sitting in the refrigerator (to a dip consistency), when made with the following ingredients. If you want a thinner dressing, add more water.

1 1/4 cups water, more if necessary

1/4 cup fresh lemon juice

1 large clove garlic

1 cup raw cashews, unsoaked

1/3 cup macadamia nuts, unsoaked (or hemp seeds)

3/4 teaspoon Himalayan crystal salt

1 teaspoon onion powder

1/4 teaspoon celery seed

2 tablespoons fresh rosemary, chopped (or more!)

Blend all of the ingredients, except the fresh rosemary, until creamy. (If you don't have a high-speed blender, you might want to grind the nuts in your food processor first. Then, transfer them to the blender with the rest of the ingredients, except the rosemary, and blend until creamy.) Add the fresh rosemary and pulse to incorporate. Rosemary Ranch Dressing/Dip recipe freezes well.

Comfort-Time Sweet Brose

This recipe is delicious, filling, high in nutrients, and everyone loves it. The delightful mixture of dried cherries, dates, various nuts and seeds, plus the seasoning = major comfort food.

1/2 cup raw pecans

1/2 cup raw pumpkin seeds

1/2 cup water, more if needed

1/2 cup soft dates, pitted and packed (approximately 8–9 dates)

3 tablespoons dried (bing) cherries, soaked 30 minutes in enough water to cover (reserve the soak water)

1/8 teaspoon cinnamon

pinch Himalayan crystal salt

1 teaspoon vanilla extract

1/2 teaspoon pumpkin pie spice

1/2 cup raw macadamia nuts, unsoaked

1/4 cup currants

1/4 cup dried cranberries

1/3 cup dried coconut, shredded and unsweetened

1/2 cup hemp seeds

1 heaping tablespoon raw cacao nibs, optional

Place the pecans in a bowl and cover with enough water by about an inch. Let them soak for 6–8 hours. Drain off the water and give them a quick rinse. Give them a light chop with your knife to make them more bite-sized. Place the pumpkin seeds in a bowl and cover with enough water by about an inch. Let them soak for 6–8 hours. Drain off the water and give them a quick rinse.

Place the water in your blender. Loosely separate the dates and add them along with the dried cherries, dried cherries soak water, cinnamon, salt, vanilla extract, and pumpkin pie spice to the blender. Blend until smooth to make a paste (add a little more water if necessary).

In your food processor, using the "S" blade, grind the macadamia nuts until they are coarsely ground. Transfer to a large bowl. Add the remaining ingredients to the macadamia nuts and toss to mix. Add the date mixture to the bowl and stir it all together with a rubber spatula until the date mixture is evenly distributed over the nut/seed mixture (or, for sticky fun, use your hands!). Stored in an airtight container, this will last up to three days.

Banana Nut Kale Salad

Yield 2–4 servings
(depending on serving size)

I can't help but sing the praises of kale. With every bite I imagine the powers of kale's nutrients making my cells stronger. Kale, itself, is a lovely shade of green that is perfect during the holiday season. But, if you want to make this salad more festive, then replace the kale with red chard, which is a gorgeous bright green leaf with red veins running throughout.

1 large bunch curly kale

2 tablespoons raw olive oil or hemp oil

2 tablespoons fresh lemon juice

1/4 teaspoon Himalayan crystal salt (or more)

pinch nutmeg

1/2 cup raw walnuts or pecans, chopped

3 medium–large bananas

Destem the kale. You can leave the more tender parts of the stem (toward the top of each leaf) in the salad, but the harder stems toward the bottom of each leaf should be torn out. Use a knife to chop into small pieces.

Place the kale into a large bowl. Add the oil, lemon juice, salt, and nutmeg. Massage the mixture thoroughly (a minute or two), and you'll notice the kale shrinking in size and getting juicy. Add the nuts and toss to mix. Before serving, add 1 banana (peeled and sliced) to each plate.

Easy Red & Green Salad

Yield 2 servings

Who doesn't love a super easy salad that takes just minutes to throw together and tastes fresh and chock full of nutrition? With the busy holiday season, sometimes easy-to-make salads are just what are in order. Enter: Easy Red & Green Salad.

It's also *perfect* for the holidays because of the beautiful holiday colors: red and green!

1 medium–large avocado, pitted, peeled & diced

15 grape or cherry tomatoes, halved or quartered*

3 medium–large leaves fresh basil, minced

juice of 1 fresh lemon**

pinch Himalayan crystal salt

pinch black pepper

Toss all of the ingredients gently in a bowl and serve.

* If you're really short on time, just add the grape (or cherry) tomatoes whole. Skip the step of halving or quartering them.

** If your lemon is large and juicy, then you might want to just squeeze half of it onto the salad. If it is small or slightly dry, then use the whole lemon. Alternatively, you can use fresh lime or orange juice… yum!

Holiday Not-Meatloaf

This recipe is beautiful, filling, and the flavors are fantastic. It's the perfect meat replacement any time of the year!

- **2 cups raw walnuts**

- **2 cups raw pecans**

- **1/4 cup + 2 tablespoons raw olive oil**

- **1 teaspoon truffle oil**

- **2 cloves garlic, minced**

- **1 1/2 tablespoons fresh lemon juice**

- **1/2 tablespoon fresh ginger, grated**

- **1 1/4 teaspoons poultry seasoning**

- **1 teaspoon Chinese 5-spice**

- **1 teaspoon dried tarragon**

- **1 teaspoon Himalayan crystal salt**

- **3/4 teaspoon cumin seed**

- **1 cup celery, diced**

- **1 cup zucchini, diced**

- **1 cup red bell pepper, diced**

- **1/2 cup fresh parsley, minced**

- **1 tablespoon red onion, minced**

Place the walnuts and pecans in a bowl and cover with enough water by about an inch. Let them soak for 6–8 hours. Drain off the water and give them a quick rinse.

Use a food processor, fitted with the "S" blade, to process the nuts, oils, garlic, lemon juice, ginger, poultry seasoning, Chinese 5-spice, tarragon, salt, and cumin seed until fairly smooth. Transfer to a large bowl. Add the remaining ingredients and stir to mix.

Take 1/3 of the mixture and put it back into the food processor, fitted with the "S" blade. Briefly process the mixture to incorporate the ingredients and chop any chunks of vegetables into smaller pieces, which you still want to show somewhat because it showcases multiple colors. Transfer this processed mixture to a new large bowl. Continue this process until you have all of the mixture processed in this fashion.

At this point, you can eat it plain or stuffed into a seeded bell pepper or tomato. For a "meatloaf" experience, spread the mixture onto a dehydrator tray, lined with a non-stick ParaFlexx sheet, and form it into a square that is the approximate size of 11 inches by 11 inches and approximately 1/2 inch high. Dehydrate at 135 degrees F for 60–75 minutes. Lower the temperature of the dehydrator to 105 degrees F and dehydrate another 4–6 hours. Flip the mixture onto a mesh dehydrator tray and peel off the ParaFlexx sheet. Dehydrate another 4–8 hours (or more, depending on your preference of texture). Cut into nine squares and serve.

Chapter 4

Fabulous Desserts

"Enthusiasm is the great hill-climber."

— ELBERT HUBBARD

Holiday desserts – does it ever get much better than that? It's one of the best parts of the season. The following are recipes that will truly make you the star of any family gathering or office party. The flavors are fantastic, but that is not all… you will feel proud after serving (and eating!) them.

Oktoberfest Raw German Chocolate Brownies

Yield 8 × 8 glass baking dish

I gave out samples of these at Whole Foods to celebrate Oktoberfest. It was so cute having people come back for seconds and thirds (one person even tried to buy my free samples from me – *ha ha*). I continue to get compliments on this recipe from fellow bloggers and customers all the time. They are truly decadent and delicious!

The Frosting

3 cups raw walnuts

1 3/4 cups dried coconut, shredded and unsweetened

3/4 cup raw agave nectar

1 tablespoon coconut oil

1 tablespoon vanilla extract

1 tablespoon coconut extract

pinch Himalayan crystal salt

The Brownie Base

1/4 cup whole raw oats

2 1/4 cups raw pecans

2/3 cup raw chocolate powder

3 tablespoons coconut oil

dash Himalayan crystal salt

3/4 teaspoon vanilla extract

1 tablespoon coconut extract

13 soft dates, pitted

1/4 cup raisins

The Frosting Directions

Take 1 cup of the walnuts and chop them with a knife. Set them in a large bowl. Add the coconut to the chopped nuts and toss briefly to mix. Take the remaining 2 cups of walnuts and grind them in a food processor, fitted with the "S" blade, until coarsely ground. Add the agave nectar, coconut oil, vanilla and coconut extracts, and salt to the food processor and process until thoroughly mixed (almost creamy-like). Transfer the mixture from the food processor to the large bowl with chopped nuts and coconut. Stir together by hand. Set aside while you make the brownie base.

The Brownie Base Directions

Grind the oats to a fine grind with a coffee grinder or blender. Transfer them to your food processor, fitted with the "S" blade. Add the pecans and process until coarsely ground. Add the chocolate powder, coconut oil, salt, vanilla and coconut extracts. Process until well incorporated. Add the dates and raisins and process until the mixture begins to stick together when pressed between two of your fingers. Press firmly into an 8 × 8 glass baking dish. Top the brownies with the frosting. Chill 1 hour before cutting and serving. This recipe freezes well.

"I Can't Believe It's Raw" Pumpkin Pie

Yield 9-inch pie

There really isn't anything else to say… *the name of the recipe says it all!*

The Crust

2 cups raw pecans

1/2 cup raisins

pinch nutmeg

The Filling

2/3 cup raw pecans

3/4 cup raw cashews

1/2 cup water

1/2 cup coconut oil

1/2 cup + 2 tablespoons raw agave nectar

4 dates, pitted, soaked 30 minutes, and drained

1 1/2 tablespoons pumpkin pie spice

1 teaspoon vanilla extract

1/4 teaspoon maple extract

5 cloves, crushed

2 pinches turmeric

dash Himalayan crystal salt

2 1/2 cups chopped carrots

2 tablespoons soy lecithin (for details, see Appendix A)

The Crust Directions

Using your food processor, fitted with the "S" blade, process the pecans until they are coarsely ground. Add the raisins and nutmeg and continue processing until the mixture begins to stick together when pressed between two of your fingers. Press the crust firmly into the bottom of an 8 or 9-inch round glass pie dish or spring form pan. Place the crust in the freezer while you make the filling.

The Filling Directions

Place the pecans in a bowl and cover with enough water by about an inch. Let them soak for 6–8 hours. Drain off the water and give them a quick rinse. Place the cashews in a bowl and cover with enough water by about an inch. Let them soak for 1–2 hours. Drain off the water and give them a quick rinse.

Using a blender, blend the cashews, pecans, water and coconut oil until creamy. Add the agave, dates, pumpkin pie spice, vanilla and maple extracts, cloves, turmeric and salt to the blender and blend until incorporated.

Add the carrots and blend until smooth. Add the soy lecithin and blend briefly until incorporated. Pour the mixture on top of the piecrust and smooth the top with a small offset spatula.

Place the pie in the freezer to set for an hour or so. Transfer to the refrigerator until you're ready to eat. "I Can't Believe It's Raw" Pumpkin Pie will stay fresh when stored in an airtight container in the refrigerator for up to a week (or 6–12 months in the freezer.

"Deck the Halls" Pistachio Cranberry Cookies

"Deck the Halls" Pistachio Cranberry Cookies (shown with Creamy Dreamy Eggless Nog, Chapter 2)

I love these cookies. They're easy, delicious and really pretty with the combination of colors from the pistachio nuts, macadamia nuts and cranberries. It's almost impossible to eat just one.

1 1/4 cups raw macadamia nuts

3/4 cup raw pistachio nuts

1/3 cup dried coconut, shredded and unsweetened

pinch Himalayan crystal salt

2 cups dried cranberries

3/4 cup raisins

Process the macadamia nuts, pistachio nuts, coconut and salt in a food processor, fitted with the "S" blade, until coarsely ground. Add the dried cranberries and raisins and continue processing until the mixture begins to stick together when pressed between your fingers. Roll the mixture into balls and then gently flatten them so they are like cookies. If desired, sprinkle dried coconut on top. These freeze well.

Sweet Pomegranate Cheesecake

Yield one 8 or 9-inch springform pan

This exquisite cheesecake is sure to please your Raw and non-Raw family and friends. Even though the cheesecake doesn't have fresh pomegranates in it, I like to garnish each slice with pomegranate seeds when they're in season. During other times of the year, I serve it without garnish. Either way… it's awesome!

The Crust

1 cup raw walnuts

1/2 cup goji berries

1 cup hemp seeds

2 tablespoons raw agave nectar

The Filling

3 cups raw cashews

3/4 cup raw agave nectar

2/3 cup coconut oil

1/2 cup fresh lemon juice

6 1/2 tablespoons pomegranate powder*

1/4 cup coconut butter

2 tablespoons lucuma powder*

2 teaspoons vanilla extract

pinch Himalayan crystal salt

2 tablespoons soy lecithin (optional)

The Crust Directions

Grind the walnuts to a coarse grind, using a food processor fitted with the "S" blade. Add the goji berries and process to mix and break apart some of the berries. Add the hemp seeds and briefly process to incorporate. Add the agave nectar and process until the mixture holds together when pressed between two of your fingers. Press the crust mixture firmly into the bottom of a springform pan and place in the freezer while you make the filling.

The Filling Directions

Place the cashews in a bowl and cover with enough water by about an inch. Let them soak for 1–2 hours. Drain off the water and give them a quick rinse.

Using a food processor, fitted with the "S" blade, process all of the ingredients, except the soy lecithin, until smooth and creamy. This could take 5–7 minutes and include stopping the processor a few times to scrape down the sides. Add the soy lecithin and process briefly to mix. Pour the filling on top of the crust. Place in the refrigerator (or freezer) to set for 1–2 hours. Stored in an airtight container in the refrigerator, Sweet Pomegranate Cheesecake will stay fresh for up to 1 week (or 6–12 months in the freezer).

* Both pomegranate and lucuma powders are available at NavitasNaturals.com

Ginger Snap Ice Cream

One bite of this amazing ice cream and you'll instantly be reminded of ginger snaps!

Ginger is an amazing and super healthy ingredient. It's beneficial for aiding circulation and digestion, and it is a rich source of antioxidants. Cloves are considered an important spice for energy circulation in Asian medicine. Cloves are also known for fighting bacteria and viruses. Some of the nutrients in cloves include: calcium, phytosterols, potassium, and manganese.

1 cup raw cashews, unsoaked

1/2 cup raw macadamia nuts, unsoaked

meat from 1 young Thai coconut

3/4 cup young Thai coconut water

1/2 cup + 2 tablespoons raw agave nectar

1 tablespoon fresh ginger, grated, packed

2 cloves, crushed

1 teaspoon vanilla extract

1/2 teaspoon powdered ginger

1/4 teaspoon allspice

1/2 teaspoon cinnamon

pinch cardamom

Grind the cashews and macadamia nuts in a food processor, fitted with the "S" blade, until finely ground. Place the remaining ingredients in a blender, add the ground nut mixture and blend until creamy. Freeze in a shallow airtight container, or use an ice cream maker (according to the manufacturer's instructions).

Pecan Spice Delight Cookies

With each bite, you'll think... *HOLIDAYS!* I have received so many testimonials from people who love these holiday cookies, and they're a *huge* hit with kids!

1 1/2 cups raw pecans

1/2 cup dried coconut, shredded and unsweetened

1 tablespoon lucuma powder*

pinch Himalayan crystal salt

1/2 teaspoon ginger powder

1/2 teaspoon cinnamon

1/4 teaspoon nutmeg

1/2 teaspoon vanilla extract

1/2 cup raisins

10 soft dates, pitted

Process all of the ingredients, except for the raisins and dates, in a food processor, fitted with the "S" blade, until coarsely ground. Add the raisins and dates and continue processing until the mixture begins to stick together when pressed between your fingers. Roll and form into desired shapes and sizes. These freeze well.

* Available at NavitasNaturals.com. If you don't have lucuma powder, then don't let that stop you from making these delicious cookies.

Hazelnut Chocolate Snowballs

Yield 15–20 cookies

Hazelnuts contain a plant sterol that has been shown to help lower cholesterol. They also have omega-3 fatty acids, as well as potassium, magnesium, fiber, vitamin E, and phosphorus. And, raw chocolate? Whew! Don't get me started on how great this stuff is! Ok, I will – *ha ha!* Raw chocolate is bursting with antioxidants, as well as plenty of magnesium, fiber, iron, calcium, zinc, copper, vitamins A, B1, B2, B3, C, E, and more.

1/2 cup dried coconut, shredded and unsweetened

1 cup raw hazelnuts

2 tablespoons raw chocolate powder

pinch Himalayan crystal salt

3/4 teaspoon hazelnut extract

8 soft dates, pitted

1/2 cup raisins

Process 1/4 cup of the coconut (reserving the other 1/4 cup for rolling the cookies in) along with the hazelnuts, chocolate and salt in a food processor, fitted with the S blade, until coarsely ground. Add the hazelnut extract, dates, and raisins. Process the mixture until it is a texture, which holds together when gently pressed between two of your fingers. Roll them into balls and then roll in the remaining coconut. These freeze well.

Variations:

- Use raw carob instead of raw chocolate.
- Replace 4 of the dates with 1/4 cup dried (bing) cherries.

Holiday Chia Pudding

Warning: The following recipe is so good that it might cause you to wake up and go to your refrigerator in the middle of the night to eat spoonful after spoonful of this pudding. It's phenomenal.

1/4 cup raw cashews

1/4 cup chia seeds

1/4 cup dried coconut, shredded and unsweetened

1 cup water

4 soft medjool dates, pitted

2 cloves

1 teaspoon lucuma powder

1/2 teaspoon powdered ginger

1/4 teaspoon vanilla extract

1/8 teaspoon cinnamon

Place the cashews in a bowl and cover with enough water by about an inch. Let them soak for 1–2 hours. Drain off the water and give them a quick rinse.

Place the chia seeds and coconut in a small bowl, briefly stir to mix, and set aside. Blend the remaining ingredients until smooth. Pour the blended cashew mixture into the bowl with the chia seeds and coconut and stir. Wait a few minutes and stir again. (The chia seeds take on a gelatinous texture.) Wait a few minutes, again, and stir. Do the "wait and stir" once more, and place the Holiday Chia Pudding in the refrigerator for about 15–20 minutes (or longer).

Yield 8 × 8 glass baking dish

This is one of my favorite Raw recipes ever. The squishy and delicious cherries explode with flavor in your mouth. It's almost impossible to only have one serving. Go ahead and try!

The Crumble

1 cup raw macadamia nuts

1 1/2 cups raw pecans

1/2 cup dried coconut, shredded and unsweetened

dash Himalayan crystal salt

1/4 cup goji berries

1/2 cup dried (bing) cherries

6 soft dates, pitted

The Cherry Filling

3 bags frozen cherries, thawed

1/2 cup dried (bing) cherries, packed

5 soft dates, pitted

1 1/2 tablespoons raw agave nectar

1 teaspoon cherry extract

The Crumble Directions

Using a food processor, fitted with the "S" blade, process the nuts, coconut, and salt until coarsely ground. Add the goji berries, dried cherries and dates and process until the mixture begins to barely stick together when gently pressed between two fingers.

The Filling Directions

Place two of the three bags of thawed cherries in a bowl. Blend the third bag of cherries with the remaining ingredients. Pour the blended cherry mixture into the bowl with the whole cherries and stir to mix.

The Assembly

Place 1/2–2/3 of the crumble mixture into the 8 × 8 glass baking dish. Gently, but firmly press it in. Pour the cherry filling on top of the pressed crumble. Sprinkle the remaining cobbler crumble on top of the filling, allowing some of the filling to peek through.

Variations:

- Serve this warm for the ultimate comfort food. Warm in your dehydrator for 30–45 minutes at 130 degrees F.
- Add chocolate! Who doesn't love the chocolate cherry combo? Add 1–2 tablespoons (or more!) of raw chocolate powder to both the crumble and the filling and/or add cacao nibs to the crumble when processing the nuts.

Green Monkey Mousse

Yield 2 1/2 cups

Here is a fun recipe that can be served as a breakfast, snack, or dessert. Green Monkey Mousse is a great dish for all of your holiday out-of-town guests (kids and adults!). It's a great holiday color (green), and if you want to make it even more holiday-like, then top each serving with either some goji berries or dried cranberries.

Avocados are filled with dietary fiber, B-vitamins (including folate), as well as lutein, vitamin A, potassium, and beta-carotene.

1/4 cup water

1 medium–large avocado, pitted and peeled

1 banana, peeled

3 tablespoons fresh lemon or lime juice

1/4 cup raw agave nectar or Date Paste (see recipe, Appendix A)

2 teaspoons lucuma powder*

1/4 teaspoon vanilla extract

pinch Himalayan crystal salt

Blend all of the ingredients until smooth and creamy. Serve immediately.

* Lucuma powder is available from NavitasNaturals.com. If you don't have lucuma powder on hand, then don't let that stop you from making this dish. Lucuma powder adds a little extra soft sweetness to it, but it'll still be good without it.

Raw Basics

This "Raw Basics" appendix is a brief introduction to Raw for those who are new to the subject. It is the same in all of my recipe books.

Why Raw?

Living the Raw vegan lifestyle has made me a more effective person… in everything I do. I get to experience pure, sustainable all-day-long energy. My body is in perfect shape and I gain strength and endurance in my exercise routine with each passing day. My relationships are the best they've ever been, because I'm happy and I love myself and my life. My headaches have ceased to exist, and my skin glows with the radiance of brand new life, which is exactly how I feel. Raw vegan is the best thing that has ever happened to me.

Whatever your passion is in life (family, business, exercise, meditation, hobbies, etc.), eating Raw vegan will take it to unbelievable new heights. Raw vegan food offers you the most amazing benefits – physically, mentally, and spiritually. It is *the* ideal choice for your food consumption if you want to become the healthiest and best "you" possible. Raw vegan food is for people who want to live longer while feeling younger. It's for people who want to feel vibrant and alive, and want to enjoy life like never before. All I ever have to say to someone is, "Just try it for yourself." It will change your life. From simple to gourmet, there's always something for everyone, and it's delicious. Come into the world of Raw with me, and experience for yourself the most amazing health *ever*.

Are you ready for your new lease on life? The time is now. Let's get started!

Some Great Things to Know Before Diving into These Recipes

Organic Food

According to the Organic Trade Association, "Organic agricultural production benefits the environment by using earth-friendly agricultural methods and practices." Here are some facts that show why organic farming is "the way to grow."

Choosing organically grown foods is one of the most important choices we can make. According to Environmental Working Group, "The growing consensus among scientists is that small doses of some pesticides and other chemicals can cause lasting damage to human health, especially during fetal development and early childhood."

I use organic produce and products for pretty much everything when it comes to my food. There are very few exceptions, and that would be if the recipe called for something I just can't get organic such as jicama, certain seasonings, or any random ingredient that my local health food store is not able to procure from an organic grower for whatever reason.

If you think organic foods are too expensive, then start in baby steps and buy a few things at a time. Realize that you're probably going to spend less money in the long run on health problems as your health improves, and going organic is one way to facilitate that.

The more people who choose organic, the lower the prices will be in the long run. Until then, if people complain about the prices of organic produce, all I can say is, "Your health is worth it!" Personally, I'm willing to spend more on it and sacrifice other things in my life if necessary. I don't need the coolest car on the block, I want the healthiest food going into my body. I like what Alice Waters says, "Why wouldn't you want to spend most of your money on food? Food is nourishment and good health. It is the most important thing in life, really."

Vote with your dollar! Here is something I do to help further this cause and you can, too. When I eat at a restaurant I always write on the bill, "I would eat here more if you served organic food." Can you imagine what would happen if we all did this?

Bottom Line: It is essential to use organic ingredients for many reasons:

1. The health benefits – superior nutrition, reduced intake of chemicals and heavy metals and decreased exposure to carcinogens. Organic food has been shown to have up to 300% more nutrition than conventionally grown, non-organic produce. And, a very important note for pregnant women: pesticides could cross the placenta and get to the growing life inside of you. Make organics an extra priority if you are pregnant.

2. To have the very best tasting food ever – use organic ingredients! I've had people tell me in my raw food demonstration classes that they never knew vegetables tasted so good – and one of the main reasons is because I only use organic.

3. Greater variety of heirloom fruits and vegetables is the result of growing organic produce.

4. Cleaner rivers and waterways for our earth and its inhabitants, along with minimized topsoil erosion. Overall, organic farming builds up the soil better, reduces carbon dioxide from the air, and has many environmental benefits.

Going Organic on a Budget

Going organic on a budget is not impossible. Here are things to keep in mind that will help you afford it:

1. Buy in bulk. Ask the store you frequent if they'll give you a deal for buying certain foods by the case. (Just make sure it's a case of something that you can go through in a timely fashion so it doesn't go to waste). Consider this for bananas or greens especially if you drink lots of smoothies or green juice, like I do.

2. See if local neighbors, family or friends will share the price of getting cases of certain foods. When you do this, you can go beyond your local grocery store and contact great places (which deliver nationally) such as Boxed Greens (BoxedGreens.com) or Diamond Organics (DiamondOrganics.com). Maybe they'll extend a discount if your order goes above a certain amount or if you get certain foods by the case. It never hurts to ask.

3. Pay attention to organic foods that are not very expensive to buy relative to the conventional prices (bananas, for example). Load up on those.

4. Be smart when picking what you buy as organic. Some conventionally grown foods have higher levels of pesticides than others. For those,go organic. Then, for foods that are not sprayed as much, you can go conventional. Avocados, for example, aren't sprayed too heavily so you could buy those as conventional. Here is a resource that keeps an updated list:

5. foodnews.org/walletguide.php

6. Buy produce that is on sale. Pay attention to which organic foods are on sale for the week and plan your menu around that. Every little bit adds up!

7. Grow your own sprouts. Load up on these for salads, soups, and smoothies. Very inexpensive. Buy the organic seeds in the bulk bins at your health food store or buy online and grow them yourself. Fun!

8. Buy organic seeds/nuts in bulk online and freeze. Nuts and seeds typically get less expensive when you order in bulk from somewhere like Sun Organic (SunOrganic.com). Take advantage of this and freeze them (they'll last the year!). Do the same with dried fruits/dates/etc. And remember, when you make a recipe that calls for expensive nuts, you can often easily replace them with a less expensive seed such as sunflower or pumpkin seeds.

9. Buy seasonally; hence, don't buy a bunch of organic berries out of season (i.e., eat more apples and bananas in the fall and winter). Also, consider buying frozen organic fruits, specially when they're on sale!

10. Be content with minimal variety from time to time. Organic spinach banana smoothies are inexpensive. You can change it up for fun by adding cinnamon one day, nutmeg another, vanilla extract yet another. Another inexpensive meal or snack is a spinach apple smoothie. Throw in a date or some raisins for extra pizazz. It helps the budget when you make salads, smoothies, and soups with ingredients that tend to be less expensive such as carrots (year round), bananas (year round), zucchini and cucumbers (in the summer), etc.

Kristen Suzanne's Tip: A Note About Herbs

Hands down, fresh herbs taste the best and have the highest nutritional value. While I recommend fresh herbs whenever possible, you can substitute dried herbs if necessary. But do so in a ratio of:

3 parts fresh to 1 part dried

Dried herbs impart a more concentrated flavor, which is why you need less of them. For instance, if your recipe calls for three tablespoons of fresh basil, you'll be fine if you use one tablespoon of dried basil instead.

The Infamous Salt Question: What Kind Do I Use?

All life on earth began in the oceans, so it's no surprise that organisms' cellular fluids chemically resemble sea water. Saltwater in the ocean is "salty" due to many, many minerals, not just sodium chloride. We need these minerals, not coincidentally, in roughly the same proportion that they exist in… guess where?… the ocean! (You've just gotta love Mother Nature.)

So when preparing food, I always use sea salt, which can be found at any health food store. Better still is sea salt that was deposited into salt beds before the industrial revolution started spewing toxins into the world's waterways. My personal preference is Himalayan Crystal Salt, fine granules. It's mined high in the mountains from ancient sea-beds, has a beautiful pink color, and imparts more than 84 essential minerals into your diet. You can use either the Himalayan crystal variety or Celtic Sea Salt, but I would highly recommend sticking to at least one of these two. You can buy Himalayan crystal salt through KristensRaw.com/store.

Kristen Suzanne's Tip: Start Small with Strong Flavors

Flavors and Their Strength

There are certain flavors and ingredients that are particularly strong, such as garlic, ginger, onion, and salt. It's important to observe patience here, as these are flavors that can be loved or considered offensive, depending on who is eating the food. I know people who want the maximum amount of salt called for in a recipe and I know some who are highly sensitive to it. Therefore, to make the best possible Raw experience for you, I recommend starting on the "small end" especially with ingredients like garlic, ginger, strong savory herbs and seasonings, onions (any variety), citrus, and even salt. If I've given you a range in a recipe, for instance *1/4–1/2 teaspoon Himalayan crystal salt* then I recommend starting with the smaller amount, and then tasting it. If you don't love it, then add a little more of that ingredient and taste it again. Start small. It's worth the extra 60 seconds it might take you to do this. You might end up using less, saving it for the next recipe you make and voila, you're saving a little money.

Lesson #1: It's very hard to correct any flavors of excess, so start small and build.

Lesson #2: Write it down. When an ingredient offers a "range" for itself, write down the amount you liked best. If you use an "optional" ingredient, make a note about that as well.

One more thing to know about some strong flavors like the ones mentioned above… with Raw food, these flavors can intensify the finished product as each day passes. For example, the garlic in your soup, on the day you made it, might be perfect. On day two, it's still really great but a little stronger in flavor. And by day three, you might want to carry around your toothbrush or a little chewing gum!

Here Is a Tip to Help Control This

If you're making a recipe in advance, such as a dressing or soup that you won't be eating until the following day or even the day after that, then hold off on adding some of the strong seasonings until the day you eat it (think garlic and ginger). Or, if you're going to make the dressing or soup in advance, use less of the strong seasoning, knowing that it might intensify on its own by the time you eat it. This isn't a huge deal because it doesn't change that dramatically, but I mention it so you won't be surprised, especially when serving a favorite dish to others.

Kristen Suzanne's Tip: Doubling Recipes

More often than not, there are certain ingredients and flavors that you don't typically double in their entirety, if you're making a double or triple batch of a recipe. These are strong-flavored ingredients similar to those mentioned above (salt, garlic, ginger, herbs, seasoning, etc). A good rule of thumb is this: For a double batch, use 1.5 times the amount for certain ingredients. Taste it and see if you need the rest. For instance, if I'm making a "double batch" of soup, and the normal recipe calls for 1 tablespoon of Himalayan crystal salt, then I'll put in 1 1/2 tablespoons to start, instead of two. Then, I'll taste it and add the remaining 1/2 tablespoon, if necessary.

This same principle is not necessarily followed when dividing a recipe in half. Go ahead and simply divide in half, or by whatever amount you're making. If there is a range for a particular ingredient provided, I still recommend that you use the smaller amount of an ingredient when dividing. Taste the final product and then decide whether or not to add more.

My recipes provide a variety of yields, as you'll see below. Some recipes make 2 servings and some make 4–6 servings. For those of you making food for only yourself, then simply cut the recipes making 4–6 servings in half. Or, as I always do… I make the larger serving size and then I have enough food for a couple of meals. If a recipe yields 2 servings, I usually double it for the same reason.

Kristen Suzanne's Tip: Changing Produce

"But I made it exactly like this last time! Why doesn't it taste the same?"

Here is something you need to embrace when preparing Raw vegan food. Fresh produce can vary in its composition of water, and even flavor, to some degree. There are times I've made marinara sauce and, to me, it was the perfect level of sweetness in the finished product. Then, the next time I made it, you would have thought I added a smidge of sweetener. This is due to the fact that fresh Raw produce can have a slightly different taste from time to time when you make a recipe (only ever so slightly, so don't be alarmed). *Aahhh, here is the silver lining!* This means you'll never get bored living the Raw vegan lifestyle because your recipes can change a little in flavor from time to time, even though you followed the same recipe. Embrace this natural aspect of produce and love it for everything that it is.

This is much less of an issue with cooked food. Most of the water is taken out of cooked food, so you typically get the same flavors and experience each and every time. Boring!

Kristen Suzanne's Tip: Ripeness and Storage for Your Fresh Produce

I never use green bell peppers because they are not "ripe." This is why so many people have a hard time digesting them (often "belching" after eating them). To truly experience the greatest health, it's important to eat fruits and vegetables at their peak ripeness. Therefore, make sure you only use red, orange, or yellow bell peppers. Store these in your refrigerator.

A truly ripe banana has some brown freckles or spots on the peel. This is when you're supposed to eat a banana. Store these on your countertop away from other produce, because bananas give off a gas as they ripen, which will affect the ripening process of your other produce. And, if you have a lot of bananas, split them up. This will help prevent all of your bananas from ripening at once.

Keep avocados on the counter until they reach ripeness (when their skin is usually brown in color and if you gently squeeze it, it "gives" just a little). At this point, you can put them in the refrigerator where they'll last up to a week longer. If you keep ripe avocados on the counter, they'll only last another couple of days. Avocados, like bananas, give off a gas as they ripen, which will affect the ripening process of your other produce. Let them ripen away from your other produce. And, if you have a lot of avocados, separate them. This will help prevent all of your avocados from ripening at once.

Tomatoes are best stored on your counter. Do not put them in the refrigerator or they'll get a "mealy" texture.

Pineapple is ripe for eating when you can gently pull a leaf out of the top of it. Therefore, test your pineapple for ripeness at the store to ensure you're buying the sweetest one possible. Just pull one of the leaves out from the top. After 3 to 4 attempts on different leaves, if you can't gently take one of them out, then move on to another pineapple.

Stone fruits (fruits with pits, such as peaches, plums, and nectarines), bananas and avocados all continue to ripen after being picked.

I have produce ripening all over my house. Sounds silly maybe, but I don't want it crowded on my kitchen countertop. I move it around and turn it over daily.

For a more complete list of produce ripening tips, check out my book, *Kristen's Raw,* available at Amazon.com.

Kristen Suzanne's Tip: Proper Dehydration Techniques

Dehydrating your Raw vegan food at a low temperature is a technique that warms and dries the food while preserving its nutritional integrity. When using a dehydrator, it is recommended that you begin the dehydrating process at a temperature of 130–140 degrees F for about an hour. Then, lower the temperature to 105 degrees F for the remaining time of dehydration. Using a high temperature such as 140 degrees F, *in the initial stages of dehydration,* does not destroy the nutritional value of the food. During this initial phase, the food does the most "sweating" (releasing moisture), which cools the food. Therefore, while the temperature of the air circulating *around* the food is about 140 degrees F, the food itself is much cooler. These directions apply only when using an Excalibur Dehydrator because of their Horizontal-Airflow Drying System. Furthermore, I am happy to only recommend Excalibur dehydrators because of their first-class products and customer service. For details, visit the *Raw Kitchen Essential Tools* section of my website at KristensRaw.com/store.

My Yield and Serving Amounts Noted in the Recipes

Each recipe in this book shows an approximate amount that the recipe yields (the quantity it makes). I find that "one serving" to me might be considered two servings to someone else, or vice versa. Therefore, I tried to use an "average" when listing the serving amount. Don't let that stop you from eating a two-serving dish in one sitting, if it seems like the right amount for you. It simply depends on how hungry you are.

What Is the Difference Between Chopped, Diced, and Minced?

Chop

Chopping gives relatively uniform cuts, but doesn't need to be perfectly neat or even. You'll often be asked to chop something before putting it into a blender or food processor, which is why it doesn't have to be uniform size since it'll be getting blended or pureed.

Dice

This produces a nice cube shape, and can be different sizes, depending on which you prefer. This is great for vegetables.

Mince

This produces an even, very fine cut, typically used for fresh herbs, onions, garlic and ginger.

Julienne

This is a fancy term for long, rectangular cuts.

What Equipment Do I Need for My New Raw Food Kitchen?

I go into much more detail regarding the perfect setup for your Raw vegan kitchen in my book, *Kristen's Raw*, which is a must read for anybody who wants to learn the easy ways to succeed with living the Raw vegan lifestyle. Here are the main pieces of equipment you'll want to get you going:

1. An excellent chef's knife (6–8 inches in length – non-serrated). Of everything you do with Raw food, you'll be chopping and cutting the most, so invest in a great knife. This truly makes doing all the chopping really fun!
2. Blender
3. Food Processor (get a 7 or 10-cup or more)
4. Juicer

5. Spiralizer or Turning Slicer

6. Dehydrator – Excalibur® is the best company by far and is available at KristensRaw.com

7. Salad spinner

8. Other knives (paring, serrated)

For links to online retailers that sell my favorite kitchen tools and foods, visit KristensRaw.com/store.

Soaking and Dehydrating Nuts and Seeds

This is an important topic. When using nuts and seeds in Raw vegan foods, you'll find that recipes sometimes call for them to be "soaked" or "soaked and dehydrated." Here is the low-down on the importance and the difference between the two.

Why Should You Soak Your Nuts and Seeds?

Most nuts and seeds come packed by Mother Nature with enzyme inhibitors, rendering them harder to digest. These inhibitors essentially shut down the nuts' and seeds' metabolic activity, rendering them dormant – for as long as they need to be – until they detect a moisture-rich environment that's suitable for germination (e.g., rain). By soaking your nuts and seeds, you trick the nuts into "waking up," shutting off the inhibitors so that the enzymes can become active. This greatly enhances the nuts' digestibility for you and is highly recommended if you want to experience Raw vegan food in the healthiest way possible.

Even though you'll want to soak the nuts to activate their enzymes, before using them, you'll need to re-dry them and grind them down anywhere from coarse to fine (into a powder almost like flour), depending on the recipe. To dry them, you'll need a dehydrator. (If you don't own a dehydrator yet, then, if a recipe calls for "soaked and dehydrated," just skip the soaking part; you can use the nuts or seeds in the dry form that you bought them).

Drying your nuts (but not yet grinding them) is a great thing to do before storing them in the freezer or refrigerator (preferably in glass mason jars). They will last a long time and you'll always have them on hand, ready to use.

In my recipes, I use nuts and seeds that are "soaked and dehydrated" (that is, dry) unless otherwise stated in the directions as needing to be soaked (wet).

Some nuts and seeds don't have to follow the enzyme inhibitor rule; therefore, they don't need to be soaked. These are:

- Macadamia nuts
- Brazil nuts
- Pine nuts
- Hemp seeds
- Most cashews

An additional note… there are times when the recipe will call for soaking, even though it's for a type of nut or seed without enzyme inhibitors, such as Brazil nuts. The logic behind this is to help *soften* the nuts so they blend into a smoother texture, especially if you don't have a high-powered blender. This is helpful when making nut milks, soups and sauces.

Instructions for "Soaking" and "Soaking and Dehydrating" Nuts

"Soaking"

The general rule to follow: Any nuts or seeds that require soaking can be soaked overnight (6–10 hours). Put the required amount of nuts or seeds into a bowl and add enough water to cover by about an inch or so. Set them on your counter overnight. The following morning, or 6–10 hours after you soaked them, drain and rinse them. They are now ready to eat or use in a recipe. At this point, they need to be refrigerated in an airtight container (preferably a glass mason jar) and they'll have a shelf life of about 3 days maximum. Only soak the amount you're going to need or eat, unless you plan on dehydrating them right away.

A note about flax seeds and chia seeds… these don't need to be soaked if your recipe calls for grinding them into a powder. Some recipes will call to soak the seeds in their "whole-seed" form, before making crackers and bread, because they create a very gelatinous and binding texture when soaked. You can soak flax or chia seeds in a ratio of one-part seeds to two-parts water, and they can be soaked for as short as 1 hour and up to 12 hours. At this point, they are ready to use (don't drain them). Personally, when I use flax seeds, I usually grind them and don't soak them. It's hard for your body to digest "whole" flax seeds, even if they are soaked. It's much easier for your body to assimilate the nutrients when they're ground to a flax meal.

"Soaking and Dehydrating"

Follow the same directions for soaking. Then, after draining and rinsing the nuts, spread them out on a mesh dehydrator sheet and dehydrate them at 140 degrees F for one hour. Lower the temperature to 105 degrees F and dehydrate them until they're completely dry, which can take up to 24 hours.

Please note, all nuts and seeds called for in my recipes will always be "Raw and Organic" and "Soaked and Dehydrated" unless the recipe calls for soaking.

Almond Pulp

Some of my recipes call for "almond pulp," which is really easy to make. After making your fresh almond milk (see *Nut/Seed Milk* recipe, p. 25) and straining it through a "nut milk bag," (available at NaturalZing.com or you can use a paint strainer bag from the hardware store – much cheaper), you will find a nice, soft pulp inside the bag. Turn the bag inside out and flatten the pulp out onto a ParaFlexx dehydrator sheet with a spatula or your hand. Dehydrate the pulp at 140 degrees F for one hour, then lower the temperature to 105 degrees F and continue dehydrating until the almond pulp is dry (up to 24 hours). Break the pulp into chunks and store in the freezer until you're ready to use it. Before using the almond pulp, grind it into a flour in your blender or food processor.

Soy Lecithin

Some recipes (desserts, in particular) will call for soy lecithin, which is extracted from soybean oil. This optional ingredient is not Raw. If you use soy lecithin, I highly recommend using a brand that is "non-GMO," meaning it was processed without any genetically modified ingredients (a great brand is Health Alliance®). Soy lecithin helps your dessert (cheesecake, for example) maintain a firmer texture. That said, it is certainly not necessary. If an amount isn't suggested, a good rule of thumb is to use 1 teaspoon per 1-cup total recipe volume.

There is another lecithin option on the market, Sunflower Lecithin. This is popular for its choline content, and it's also used as an emulsifier in recipes. Soy lecithin is a common "go-to" source, but not everyone wants a soy product. That's all changed now that sunflower lecithin is available. You can find a link to purchase it at KristensRaw.com/store.

Ice Cream Flavorings

When making Raw vegan ice cream, it's better to use alcohol-free extracts so they freeze better.

Sweeteners

The following is a list of sweeteners that you might see used in my recipes. It's important to know that the healthiest sweeteners are fresh whole fruits, including fresh dates. That said, dates sometimes compromise texture in recipes. As a chef, I look for great texture, and as a health food advocate, I lean towards fresh dates. But as a consultant helping people embrace a Raw vegan lifestyle, I'm also supportive of helping them transition, which sometimes means using raw agave nectar, or some other easy-to-use sweetener that might not have the healthiest ranking in the Raw food world, but is still much healthier than most sweeteners used in the Standard American Diet.

Most of my recipes can use pitted dates in place of raw agave nectar. There is some debate among Raw food enthusiasts as to whether agave nectar is Raw. The company I primarily use (Madhava®) claims to be Raw and says they do not heat their Raw agave nectar above 118 degrees F. If however, you still want to eat the healthiest of sweeteners, then bypass the raw agave nectar and use pitted dates. In most recipes, you can simply substitute 1–2 pitted dates for 1 tablespoon of raw agave nectar. Dates will not give you a super creamy texture, but the texture can be improved by making a "date paste" (pureeing pitted and soaked dates – with their soak water, plus some additional water, if necessary – in a food processor fitted with the "S" blade). This, of course, takes a little extra time.

If using raw agave nectar is easier and faster for you, then go ahead and use it; just be sure to buy the raw version that says they don't heat the agave above 118 degrees F. And, again, if you're looking to go as far as you can on the spectrum of health, then I recommend using pitted dates. Many of my recipes use raw agave nectar because that is most convenient for people.

Raw Agave Nectar

There are a variety of agave nectars on the market, but again, not all of them are Raw. Make sure it is labeled "Raw" on the bottle *as well as claiming that it isn't processed above 118 degrees F*. Just because the label says "Raw" does not necessarily mean it is so… do a double check and make sure it also claims "not to be heated above 118 degrees F." Agave nectar is noteworthy for having a low glycemic index.

Dates

Dates are probably the healthiest of sweeteners, because they're a fresh whole food (I'm a big fan of Medjool dates). Fresh organic dates are filled with nutrition, including calcium and magnesium. I like to call dates, "Nature's Candy."

Feel free to use dates instead of agave or honey in raw vegan recipes. If a recipe calls for 1/2 cup of raw agave, then you can substitute with approximately 1/2 cup of pitted dates (or more).

You can also make a recipe of *Date Paste* to replace raw agave (or to use in combination with it). It's not always as sweet as agave, so you might want to adjust the amount according to your taste by using a bit more *Date Paste*.

Honey

Most honey is technically raw, but it is not vegan by most definitions of "vegan" because it is produced by animals, who therefore are at risk of being mistreated. While honey does not have the health risks associated with animal byproducts such as eggs or dairy, it can spike the body's natural sugar levels. Agave nectar has a lower, healthier glycemic index and can replace any recipe you find that calls for honey, in a 1 to 1 ratio.

Maple Syrup

Maple syrup is made from boiled sap of the maple tree. It is not considered raw, but some people still use it as a sweetener in certain dishes.

Rapadura®

This is a dried sugarcane juice, and it's not raw. It is, however, an unrefined and unbleached organic whole-cane sugar. It imparts a nice deep sweetness to your recipes, even if you only use a little. Feel free to omit it if you'd like to adhere to a strictly Raw program. You can substitute Rapadura with home-made date sugar (see Dates above).

Stevia

This is from the leaf of the stevia plant. It has a sweet taste and doesn't elevate blood sugar levels. It's very sweet, so you'll want to use much less stevia than you would any other sweetener. My mom actually grows her own stevia. It's a great addition in fresh smoothies, for example, to add some sweetness without the calories. When possible, the best way to have stevia is grow it yourself.

Yacon Syrup

This sweetener has a low glycemic index, making it very attractive to some people. It has a molasses-type flavor that is very enjoyable. You can replace raw agave with this sweetener, but keep in mind that it's not as sweet in flavor as raw agave nectar. The brand I usually buy is Navitas Naturals, which is available at NavitasNaturals.com. For more information, see Appendix C, Resources Section.

Sun-Dried Tomatoes

By far, the best sun-dried tomatoes are those you make yourself with a dehydrator. If you don't have a dehydrator, make sure you buy the "dry" sun-dried tomatoes, usually found in the bulk section of your health food market. Don't buy the kind that are packed in a jar of oil.

Also… don't buy sun-dried tomatoes if they're really dark (almost black) because these just don't taste as good. Again, I recommend making them yourself if you truly want the freshest flavor possible. It's really fun to do!

Eating with Your Eyes

Most of us, if not all, naturally eat with our eyes before taking a bite of food. So, do yourself a favor and make your eating experience the best ever with the help of a simple, gorgeous presentation. Think of it this way, with real estate, it's always *location, location, location*, right? Well, with food, it's always *presentation, presentation, presentation*.

Luckily, Raw food does this on its own with all of its naturally vibrant and bright colors. But I take it even one step farther – I use my best dishes when I eat. I use my beautiful wine glasses for my smoothies and juices. I use my fancy goblets for many of my desserts. Why? Because I'm worth it. And, so are you! Don't save your good china just for company. Believe me, you'll notice the difference. Eating well is an attitude, and when you take care of yourself, your body will respond in kind.

Online Resources for Great Products

For a complete and detailed list of my favorite kitchen tools, products, and various foods (all available online), please visit: KristensRaw.com/store.

Book & DVD Recommendations

I highly recommend reading the following life-changing books and DVDs.

- *Diet for a New America*, by John Robbins
- *The Food Revolution*, by John Robbins
- *The China Study*, by T. Colin Campbell
- *Skinny Bitch*, by Rory Freedman
- *Food, Inc.* (DVD)
- *Food Matters* (DVD)
- *The Future of Food* (DVD)
- *Earthlings* (DVD)

Measurement Conversions

1 tablespoon = 3 teaspoons

1 ounce = 2 tablespoons

1/4 cup = 4 tablespoons

1/3 cup = 5 1/3 tablespoons

1 cup

= 8 ounces

= 16 tablespoons

= 1/2 pint

1/2 quart

= 1 pint

= 2 cups

1 gallon

= 4 quarts

= 8 pints

= 16 cups

= 128 ounces

Basic Recipes to Know

Nourishing Rejuvelac

Yield 1 gallon

Rejuvelac is a cheesy-tasting liquid that is rich in enzymes and healthy flora to support a healthy intestine and digestion. Get comfortable making this super easy recipe because its use goes beyond just drinking it between meals.

Some people are concerned about the wheat aspect to wheat berries being used in most Rejuvelac recipes. While many people easily tolerate Rejuvelac made with wheat berries in spite of having wheat intolerance issues, there are other ingredients you can use to make Rejuvelac wheat-free. Some options are buckwheat, rice, quinoa, and more.

1 cup soft wheat berries, rye berries, or a mixture

water

Place the wheat berries in a half-gallon jar and fill the jar with water. Screw the lid on the jar and soak the wheat berries overnight (10–12 hours) on your counter. The next morning, drain and rinse them. Sprout the wheat berries for 2 days, draining and rinsing 1–2 times a day.

Then, fill the jar with purified water and screw on the lid, or cover with cheesecloth secured with a rubber band. Allow to ferment for 24–36 hours, or until the desired tartness is achieved. It should have a cheesy, almost tart/lemony flavor and scent.

Strain your rejuvelac into another glass jar and store in the refrigerator for up to 5–7 days. For a second batch using the same sprouted wheat berries, fill the same jar of already sprouted berries with water again, and allow to ferment for 24 hours. Strain off the rejuvelac as you did the time before this. You can do this process yet again, noting that each time the rejuvelac gets a little weaker in flavor.

Enjoy 1/4–1 cup of *Nourishing Rejuvelac* first thing in the morning and/or between meals. It's best to start with a small amount and work your way up as your body adjusts.

Suggestion:

- For extra nutrition and incredible flavor, Nourishing Rejuvelac can be used in various recipes such as raw vegan cheeses, desserts, smoothies, soups, dressings and more. Simply use it in place of the water required by the recipe.

Nut/Seed Milk (regular)

Yield 4–5 cups

The creamiest nut/seed milk traditionally comes from hemp seeds, cashews, pine nuts, Brazil nuts or macadamia nuts, although I'm also a huge fan of milks made from walnuts, pecans, hazelnuts, almonds, sesame seeds, sunflower seeds, and pumpkin seeds.

This recipe does not include a sweetener, but when I'm in the mood for a little sweetness, I add a couple of pitted dates or a squirt of raw agave nectar. Yum!

1 1/2 cups raw nuts or seeds

3 1/4 cups water

pinch Himalayan crystal salt, optional

Place the nuts in a bowl and cover with enough water by about an inch. Let them soak for 6-8 hours (unless you're using cashews, pine nuts, Brazil nuts, or macadamia nuts, in which case you only have to soak them about an hour. Hemp seeds do not need soaking because they're very soft and easy to blend, but adjust the amount of water used in the recipe, as needed). Drain off the water and give them a quick rinse.

Blend the ingredients until smooth and deliciously creamy. For an even *extra creamy* texture, strain your nut/seed milk through a nut milk bag.

My Basic Raw Mayonnaise

Yield about 2 1/2 cups

People tell me all the time how much they like this recipe.

1 cup raw cashews

1/2 teaspoon paprika

2 cloves garlic

1 teaspoon onion powder

3 tablespoons fresh lemon juice

1/4 cup extra virgin olive oil or hemp oil

2 tablespoons parsley, chopped

2 tablespoons water, if needed

Place the cashews in a bowl and cover with enough water by about an inch. Let them soak for 1 hour. Drain off the water and give them a quick rinse.

Blend all of the ingredients, except the parsley, until creamy. Pulse in the parsley. *My Basic Raw Mayonnaise* will stay fresh for up to one week in the refrigerator.

Date Paste

Yield 1–1 1/4 cups

It's great to keep this on hand in the refrigerator so you have it available and ready to use. *Date Paste* is easy to make and should take you less than 10 minutes to prepare once your dates are soaked. Store it in an airtight container in the refrigerator (a glass mason jar is perfect).

15 medjool dates, pitted, soaked 15 minutes (reserve soak water)

1/4–1/2 cup reserved "soak water"

Using a food processor, fitted with the "S" blade, puree the ingredients until you have a smooth paste.

Raw Mustard

Yield approximately 1 cup

2 teaspoons yellow mustard seeds, soaked 1–2 hours, then drained

1/2 cup extra virgin olive oil or hemp oil

1 tablespoon dry mustard powder

1 tablespoon apple cider vinegar

1 tablespoon fresh lemon juice or lime juice

1/4 cup raw agave nectar

1/2 teaspoon Himalayan crystal salt

1/4 teaspoon turmeric

Blend all of the ingredients together until smooth. It might be very thick, so if you want, add some water or oil to help thin it out. Adding more oil will help reduce the "heat" if it's too spicy for your taste.

Variation:

- "Honey" Mustard Version: Add more raw agave nectar (until you reach the desired sweetness).

Crème Fraiche

Yield approximately 2 cups

1 cup raw cashews

1/4–1/2 cup *Nourishing Rejuvelac* (see p. 23)

1–2 tablespoons raw agave nectar

Place the cashews in a bowl and cover with enough water by about an inch. Let them soak for 1 hour. Drain off the water and give them a quick rinse.

Blend the ingredients until smooth. Store in an airtight glass mason jar for up to 5 days. This freezes well, so feel free to make a double batch for future use.

Sweet Nut/Seed Cream (thick)

Yield 2–3 cups

1 cup raw nuts or seeds

1–1 1/2 cups water, more if needed

2–3 tablespoons raw agave nectar or 3–4 dates, pitted

1/2 teaspoon vanilla extract, optional

Place the nuts in a bowl and cover with enough water by about an inch. Let them soak for 6–8 hours (unless you're using cashews, pine nuts, Brazil nuts, or macadamia nuts, in which case you only have to soak them about an hour. Hemp seeds do not need soaking because they're very soft and easy to blend, but adjust the amount of water used in the recipe, as needed). Drain off the water and give them a quick rinse.

Blend all of the ingredients until smooth.